RRjC

AUG   2016

BIOINDICATOR SPECIES

POLAR BEARS
MATTER

by Tammy Gagne

Content Consultant
Dr. Jeff Welker
Fulbright Distinguished US Arctic Chair-Norway
Professor of Ecology, University of Alaska Anchorage

Core Library
An Imprint of Abdo Publishing
abdopublishing.com

abdopublishing.com

Published by Abdo Publishing, a division of ABDO, PO Box 398166, Minneapolis, Minnesota 55439. Copyright © 2016 by Abdo Consulting Group, Inc. International copyrights reserved in all countries. No part of this book may be reproduced in any form without written permission from the publisher. Core Library™ is a trademark and logo of Abdo Publishing.

Printed in the United States of America, North Mankato, Minnesota
072015
012016

Cover Photo: Sergey Uryadnikov/Shutterstock Images
Interior Photos: Sergey Uryadnikov/Shutterstock Images, 1, 10; John Pitcher/iStockphoto, 4; Kenneth Canning/iStockphoto, 6, 43; Shutterstock Images, 9; Josef Friedhuber/iStockphoto, 12, 45; Dorling Kindersley/Thinkstock, 14; iStockphoto, 16, 21 (top), 21 (middle top), 21 (middle), 36; Hung Chung Chih/Shutterstock Images, 18; Alex Raths/iStockphoto, 21 (middle bottom); Nancy Nehring/iStockphoto, 21 (bottom); Flip Nicklin/Minden Pictures/Newscom, 22, 34; Paul Nicklen/National Geographic, 24; Dan Guravich/Corbis, 27; Paul Goldstein/Exodus/Rex Features/AP Images, 28; Daniel J. Cox/Corbis, 30; Jenny E. Ross/Corbis, 32; Steve Kazlowski/ Danita Delimont Photography/Newscom, 38

Editor: Jon Westmark
Series Designer: Laura Polzin

Library of Congress Control Number: 2015945400

Cataloging-in-Publication Data
Gagne, Tammy.
 Polar bears matter / Tammy Gagne.
  p. cm. -- (Bioindicator species)
ISBN 978-1-68078-013-0 (lib. bdg.)
Includes bibliographical references and index.
1. Polar bears--Juvenile literature. 2. Polar bear ecology--Juvenile literature. 3. Environmental protection--Juvenile literature. I. Title.
599.786--dc23

                                                                    2015945400

CONTENTS

CHAPTER ONE

ARE POLAR BEARS IN TROUBLE?

A tired and hungry polar bear climbs ashore from the icy waters of the Arctic Ocean. The bear has returned to solid ground after a winter of hunting seals on sea ice. Just a few weeks ago, this part of the Arctic was frozen solid. But the summer warmth has turned much of sea ice to water. The melting forced the polar bear to make a decision. It could stay on the ice or swim to land in search of

Polar bears spend time both on land and on sea ice.

Polar bears cannot hunt seals effectively without sufficient amounts of sea ice.

food. This time of the year is known as the fasting period for polar bears. Without many seals to feast on, the bears survive mainly off the fat they have stored in their bodies.

In the last few decades, though, the ice has been melting earlier. This change has left polar bears with less time to harvest seals on the sea ice and build up fat. The bears must find other food sources in order to survive. This change in routine tells a lot about what is happening to the Arctic ecosystem.

Polar bears are bioindicator animals. Bioindicators are plants or animals scientists study to better understand the health of an ecosystem. The problems polar bears face can help people understand worldwide problems, such as climate change.

Polar bears can also teach humans about the effects of pollution. When a polar bear eats a seal, the bear does not consume just the meat. The bear also eats substances that have built up in the seal's body. Seals live in water. And their bodies take in whatever is in the water, including dangerous chemicals from pollution. The effects of these chemicals can become apparent in polar bears. This means the health of polar bears can indicate whether other animals in the ecosystem are also suffering.

Threats to Polar Bears

Polar bears are the top land predators of the Arctic. They can weigh up to 1,600 pounds (726 kg). And they can easily overpower most other animals. Their huge front paws make them strong swimmers. Some polar bears have been known to travel hundreds of miles from land in search of food.

Even strong swimmers have limits, though. Polar bears must return to land in spring before too much ice has melted. If they stay on the ice too long, they might not be able to survive the long swim.

Bears that leave the ice too early face different problems. They do not have as much fat stored up from eating seals. These bears must find food on land. They might eat whale carcasses, geese, or berries.

Polar bears hunt seals by waiting for them to surface.

Polar bear cubs depend on their mother for survival for approximately two years.

The early arrival of polar bears tells humans many things about what is happening to the Arctic. First it shows that climate change is causing animals to change their most basic ways of life, such as what they eat and where they go. One might think polar bears can get enough food from sources other than seals. But polar bears need the fat from seal meat to stay healthy.

Melting ice also makes it difficult for polar bears to reproduce. Only strong females can give birth to healthy cubs.

PERSPECTIVES
Warming's Effect on Native People

Native people living in the Arctic have long survived by hunting. But warming temperatures have caused sea ice to melt in areas where hunters have hunted seals for generations. In many cases, the warmer air has turned once sturdy sea-ice routes into dangerous terrain. One of the biggest risks is thinning ice. Hunters and their sleds can fall through ice where it was once solid. Thinner ice has made hunters turn to sources of food available on land, such as caribou, musk oxen, and salmon. The changing climate has also shortened the hunting season. This means native people must find food in less time.

The summer sea ice melting period has become longer over the past 25 years.

Pregnant females need extra nutrition. Scientists say that if the ice starts melting just one month earlier, as many as 73 percent of female polar bears would not complete their pregnancies and deliver cubs. If the melting begins two months earlier, there is a possibility that no new cubs would be born at all.

Struggling polar bears are a clear sign that climate change is hurting the environment. Falling polar bear numbers are an early example of the effects of rising temperatures on Earth. If people do not pay attention to this bioindicator, entire ecosystems could suffer.

A Problem for Many Nations

The polar bear's natural range is the Arctic Circle. This region includes land and water belonging to a number of countries. Polar bears can be found in Alaska, Canada, Greenland, Norway, and Russia.

The Arctic Circle is colder than many other areas of the world. But what matters to polar bears is the temperature of the water. Freshwater freezes at 32 degrees Fahrenheit (0°C). Seawater freezes at

One Thing Leads to Another

Polar bears are land animals. But they spend a lot of their time in water. Their survival affects other animals living in the Arctic Ocean. Seal populations would rise if polar bears went extinct. There would be more seals eating cod. Cod numbers would go down. This would hurt the local economy, which uses Arctic cod for food and trade.

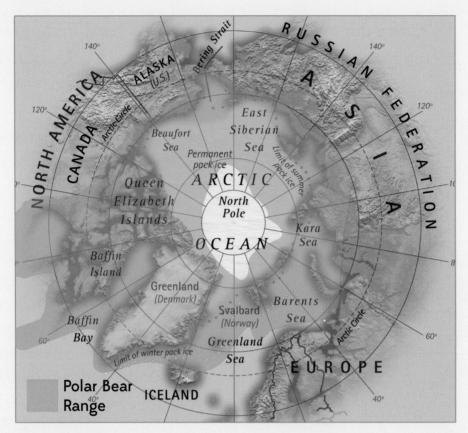

Where Polar Bears Live

Polar bears are found in five different countries around the Arctic Circle. Their natural range covers more than 1 million square miles (1.6 million sq km). How does the map compare to what you have read in the text? In what way does it help you think about polar bears differently?

28.4 degrees Fahrenheit (-2°C). The salt in seawater lowers its freezing point. This means seawater has to be colder to freeze.

Since the 1960s, the average winter temperature in the Arctic has gone up by approximately six degrees Fahrenheit (3°C). The warmer weather makes it harder for polar bears to survive. It also poses a threat to the other animals and people who rely on the polar bear for their own survival.

EXPLORE ONLINE

Go to the website below and read about what is happening to polar bears. How does this information compare to what you have read in Chapter One? Write a paragraph about why you think polar bears are a good bioindicator. Use facts to back up your opinion.

Polar Bears and Climate Change
mycorelibrary.com/polar-bears-matter

CHAPTER TWO

A COMPLEX PROBLEM

One of the biggest threats to polar bears is global warming. Global warming is the gradual rise in Earth's temperature. It is caused largely by gases humans release into the air. One of the main gases responsible for global warming is carbon dioxide (CO_2). It is known as a greenhouse gas. Greenhouse gases trap heat in the atmosphere, just as a glass ceiling traps heat inside a greenhouse.

Greenhouse gases, such as carbon dioxide, stay in the atmosphere once released.

Cars are a major contributor of greenhouse gases.

Burning fossil fuels, such as oil and coal, produces carbon dioxide. Big factories and power plants burn huge amounts of fossil fuels. But big companies are not the only problem.

People on Earth drive more than 1 billion cars. Each one releases approximately six tons (5.4 metric tons) of carbon dioxide per year. The Environmental Protection Agency (EPA) estimates that transportation is responsible for 27 percent of the greenhouse gases released into the atmosphere. This makes automobiles big contributors to global warming.

Trees and other plants take in carbon dioxide. They use it to produce oxygen. But all the trees in the world cannot keep up with the amount of carbon dioxide being released by humans. In addition, vast numbers of trees are being cut down. This is called deforestation. It has made global warming an even bigger concern.

Pollutants

Earth's population has grown steadily over time. Between 1900 and 2000, the number of people living on Earth jumped from 1.65 billion to 6 billion. Growing enough food for the people of the world is a

Changes in the Works

Shell is one of the largest oil companies in the world. And it is making big changes to lower its emissions. In the past, the company had been accused of releasing high levels of chemicals into the atmosphere. But in 2013, Shell agreed to lower emissions at its plant in Texas. The company also said it was installing a system that would give the public data on pollution levels. The EPA stated that the steps Shell is taking will significantly cut the amount of many gases linked to global warming.

PERSPECTIVES

A Rising Population?

Not all scientists agree about the state of certain bioindicators. This is the case with polar bears. Drikus Gissing is a researcher in Nunavut, a territory of northern Canada. He does not think the bear population is in trouble. Members of many native communities agree with Gissing. Hunters insist that polar bears are increasing in number. A study released in 2012 showed that the Canadian Arctic is home to approximately 15,000 polar bears. Gissing stated this number might be an all-time high for the area.

complicated task. Insects often destroy crops before they can grow food for people to eat. When this happens, farmers suffer. All the money they spent growing the food is lost along with the crops.

To solve this problem, scientists created pesticides. These powerful chemicals keep insects from eating crops. But many of these chemicals also hurt wildlife. Scientists studying polar bears have found traces of pesticides in the bodies of these animals. In many cases, the chemicals had

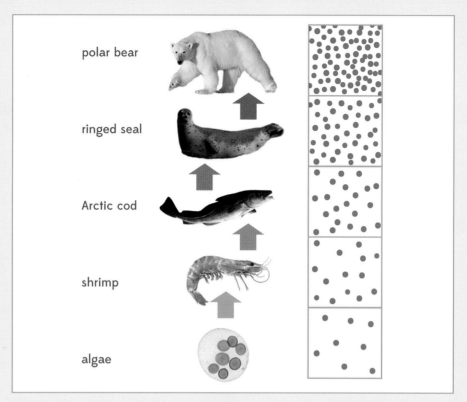

Bioaccumulation

Each time an animal eats another animal, it also takes in any pollution in the prey's body. Polar bears are at the top of the food chain. They eat animals that have eaten other animals. Therefore, polar bears consume greater concentrations of dangerous substances. If a polar bear has a lot of pollutants in its body, what can we suppose about its surroundings?

polar bear

ringed seal

Arctic cod

shrimp

algae

traveled long distances before they made it to the bears.

Oil Spills

Oil companies have also brought pollution to the Arctic. No company ever plans to spill oil. But many

Oil from the *Exxon Valdez* spreads across Prince William Sound, Alaska.

accidents have occurred. One of the best-known oil spills took place in 1989. A ship called the *Exxon Valdez* struck a reef. It dumped 11 million gallons (42 million L) of oil into Prince William Sound, Alaska. The oil spread across 3,000 square miles (7,770 sq km).

An oil spill is dangerous in the cold waters of the Arctic. The lower temperatures keep the oil highly concentrated. For this reason, animals that come into contact with the oil may take in more of the substance. Studying polar bears can tell us just how long the effects of a spill like that of the *Exxon Valdez* can last.

FURTHER EVIDENCE

Chapter Two focuses on the biggest threats to polar bear populations. What was one of the chapter's main points? What evidence was given to support that point? Check out the website at the link below. Choose a quote from the website that relates to this chapter. Does this quote support the author's main point? Does it make a new point? Write a few sentences about how the quote relates to this chapter.

Polar Bears International: Climate Change
mycorelibrary.com/polar-bears-matter

CHAPTER THREE

WHY POLAR BEARS MATTER

No one knows exactly how many polar bears are left in the world today. The bears live in remote areas. This makes them harder for scientists to study. But experts approximate the current population is between 20,000 and 25,000. If humans do not work to save polar bears, two-thirds of these animals could be gone by 2050. Within another 50 years, they could become extinct.

Researchers study a tranquilized polar bear in Nunavut, Alaska.

Enough to Go Around

The Arctic fox depends on polar bears for a certain amount of its food. Arctic foxes mainly eat tiny, fast rodents called lemmings. It takes several lemmings to give the Arctic fox enough calories to survive. But lemmings can sometimes be scarce. When an Arctic fox is unable to catch enough lemmings, it turns to the seal meat left behind by polar bears. Without polar bears' leftovers, the Arctic fox could also become threatened.

A Chain Reaction

Losing polar bears would have wide-reaching effects. Polar bears hunt seals. Without the bears, seal numbers would rise quickly. The extra seals would need food to survive. This would increase competition for food between seals and humans. As a result, sea creatures like herring, shrimp, and cod would potentially become threatened. The number of seals would then decrease. Many would die of starvation.

The problems created by climate change do not start with the polar bear's extinction, however.

Arctic foxes often eat scraps that polar bears leave behind.

Polar bears are already arriving on land too early in the spring. This affects the animals that live on land. The bears take food that would have been another animal's meal.

A polar bear sneaks up on a group of guillemot in Spitsbergen, Norway.

Some bears are killing prey before it can reach adulthood. A type of Arctic bird called the guillemot is already struggling to survive global warming. Melting ice has made it hard for the bird to reach its main food source, Arctic cod. Polar bears are placing the bird in even greater danger by eating guillemot chicks. The bird could become extinct if this continues.

How Will Humans Be Affected?

Polar bears' lifestyles are sensitive to small changes in the climate. This makes them good measures of climate change around the planet. Scientists predict that as many as one-quarter of Earth's species could face extinction if global warming is not slowed. Warming waters are already threatening some species. For example, many lobsters in southern New England are suffering from parasites due to warmer ocean waters. The problem has cut the number of lobsters that can be caught and sold in this region.

Even people living much farther south are seeing the effects of global warming. Warmer water in the tropics is killing algae. Coral reefs need this organism to stay healthy. And approximately 30 million people depend on reefs for their livelihoods.

Scientists take a blood sample from an immobilized polar bear in Kaktovik, Alaska.

Pollution is also an issue in southern regions. Water can spread pollution for many miles. Scientists studying Arctic animals have found traces of pesticides that have traveled all the way from Southeast Asia.

The ice that polar bears depend on is also an important part of life around the world. With less ice, the temperatures of Earth's oceans rise. The warmer water in turn melts the ice more quickly. This cycle could eventually destroy all the sea ice.

As water temperatures go up, ocean levels rise. This is because water expands as it gets warmer. Seawater could one day cover land that is now shoreline,

Part Polar Bear, Part Grizzly Bear

One might think polar bears in search of ice would head farther north. But as ice breaks up, it drifts southward. Polar bears can become stranded on the broken-up pieces. When polar bears drift far south, they often encounter grizzly bears. Sometimes these bears mate, producing hybrid cubs. If this continues, it could mean the end of the polar bear species.

Scientists measure sea ice in the Arctic Ocean.

including places along the Arctic coast. Hundreds of millions of people who now live within 25 feet (8 m) of sea level could lose their homes to rising waters.

It is no accident we see so many pictures of polar bears alongside information about global warming. Journalist Simon Barnes explains:

> The bear has gone right to the heart of the matter. Al Gore used the image unsparingly in his Oscar-winning documentary, An Inconvenient Truth: the white nose ploughing a furrow across the sea that leads to nowhere. And while bringing in the polar bear risks charges of sentimentality, it cannot be denied that the bears tell us, by express delivery, a truth that we can now believe with our guts as well as our minds. The bear asks us all the big questions. If the Arctic ice cap vanished and the polar bear became extinct, what will happen to the other species that live on this planet? Humans are just one of many; we can't avoid global warming by going indoors and switching up the air-conditioning.

Source: Simon Barnes. "The Bear Necessities of Survival." The Times (London) December 12, 2009, Saturday Review: 9+. Print. 9.

Back It Up

The author of this passage uses evidence to support a point. Write a paragraph describing the point the author is making. Then write down two or three pieces of evidence the author uses to make the point.

CHAPTER FOUR

LOOKING TO THE FUTURE

The best news about polar bears is that they still exist today. But humans must listen to the warnings of these bioindicators. By making important changes now, we can ensure the survival of polar bears and other Arctic species for many years to come.

A researcher attempts to weigh a squirming polar bear cub near Resolute, Canada.

Solar energy creates fewer emissions than energy from oil or coal.

Slowing Down Global Warming

We can lessen the effects of global warming by lowering the amount of carbon dioxide we put into the environment. One way to do this is by using less electricity. Power plants do not need to make as much electricity if less is being used. Lower power production means less pollution. An easy way to lower electricity use is by turning off lights and other electrical devices when they are not being used. Even one person saving electricity makes a difference. The results are even greater when big companies make an effort to conserve.

We can also reduce the amount of carbon dioxide given off by cars. One way to do this is by walking or biking instead of driving. Carpooling also helps cut emissions. We can also make a difference by using cars that release fewer emissions.

Using cleaner energy, such as solar power, also helps reduce emissions. Solar energy systems can be expensive at first, but they can save users money in the long run.

PERSPECTIVES
Different Opinions

In 1973 an international agreement limited polar bear hunting around the world. Researcher Mitch Taylor insists that more polar bears are alive today than four decades ago because of this move. Despite the species' threatened status, Taylor does not believe the bears are headed for extinction. He thinks the climate models have exaggerated the warming projections. Taylor believes the bears could survive an increase of up to 2.7 degrees Fahrenheit (1.5°C).

The Arctic National Wildlife Refuge is home to approximately 1,500 polar bears.

Joining the Cause

Organizations like the Sierra Club and Greenpeace work to help save important animals, such as the polar bear. These groups and many others tell the public about what is happening to polar bears and other animals. They also work with governments to protect nature by cutting pollution and slowing global warming.

The Arctic National Wildlife Refuge is a protected area for polar bears in the United States. Neither hunters nor oil companies are allowed to interfere with polar bears in this area. But some people think the land should be drilled for oil. Environmental groups fight large companies that want to drill in these protected areas.

What's Next?

According to the National Wildlife Federation, polar bears are in serious danger of going extinct due

Tracking Polar Bears

Scientists use radio collars to track polar bears. The devices help researchers study the animals without affecting their daily lives. The collars track where polar bears go. This information helps scientists learn how polar bears are reacting to the melting ice. But radio collars have one big drawback. They can only be used with female bears. A male polar bear's neck is wider than its head. The collars fall off of males.

to global warming. The species was added to the US Endangered Species Act as threatened in 2008. The biggest reason for this decision was the bear's shrinking territory: the melting polar ice.

The polar bears facing the greatest threat today are those living in the western Hudson Bay. This is the southernmost area of the species' range. Experts predict that if ice keeps melting, the world may lose this population of polar bears for good.

Another big concern is the dropping number of polar bear cubs. Without enough offspring, a species cannot survive. The falling birth rate may be the biggest cry for help that these bioindicators are making.

The future of the polar bear depends on how people react to the information the species offers. Making changes now may save the polar bear from extinction. It may also help save humans from the effects of global warming in the process.

Polar Bears International Chief Scientist Steven Amstrup spoke about the polar bear's situation in an interview with *National Geographic*:

> *The solution is conceptually simple. In practice, because the principal [greenhouse gas] of concern (CO_2) is so tightly linked to our economy, the challenges are difficult, but it is not correct to suggest we cannot solve this. In fact, it is counter productive to make such a suggestion. It is clear that if people and policy makers believe there is nothing they can do, they will do nothing. Therefore it is important that all media outlets present this situation in its proper light and emphasize that the loss of polar bear habitat is not unavoidable. We can change this, and I am confident that we will do so.*
>
> Source: David Braun. "Interview with Polar Bears International Chief Scientist Steven Amstrup." National Geographic Voices. National Geographic, October 7, 2010. Web. Accessed April 22, 2015.

What's the Big Idea?

What is the main idea of the above quote? What evidence does the author use to support his points? Find two or three sentences that show how he backed up his opinions.

Common Name: Polar bear

Scientific Name: *Ursus maritimus*

Average Size: 7.25 to 8 feet (2.2–2.5 m)

Average Weight: 900 to 1,600 pounds (410–726 kg)

Color: White

Average Life Span: 25 to 30 years

Diet: Ringed seals

Habitat: Arctic sea ice

Predators: None

What's Happening: Polar bear populations are decreasing.

Where It's Happening: The Arctic Circle

Why It's Happening: Arctic ice is melting earlier in the spring. Habitat loss threatens polar bears' ability to find food. This, combined with the effects of pollution, weakens polar bears and puts them at risk.

Why It's Important: The decreasing polar bear population is a sign that the environment is in trouble.

What You Can Do:

- Write a letter to your state representative. Explain the importance of polar bears as bioindicators.
- Conserve energy every day and encourage others to do so as well.
- Donate money to an environmental organization that works to protect polar bears.

Why Do I Care?

Polar bears are facing an uncertain future due to global warming. Chances are good, though, that you live far away from this bioindicator species. Make a list of all the ways that a decrease in the polar bear population could affect you and people who live in other regions of the world.

Dig Deeper

After reading this book, what questions do you still have about polar bears? Maybe you want to know what animal species are most affected by polar bears. Write down one or two questions that can guide you in your research. With the help of an adult, find a reliable source that can answer these questions. Then write a short paragraph about what you learned.

Surprise Me

Chapter One shared some interesting information about polar bears as a bioindicator species. List two or three facts from the chapter that you found most surprising. Why did these facts surprise you?

Tell the Tale

Write 200 words from the point of view of a polar bear that was forced to come ashore early due to melting ice. Make sure to set the scene, develop a sequence of events, and include a conclusion.

GLOSSARY

bioaccumulation
the increase of pollutants in an organism

conserve
to avoid wasteful use

deforestation
clearing an area of forests

ecosystem
a community of living things that affect one another and their environment

emission
something given off or discharged

extinct
no longer existing

global warming
the gradual increase in the overall temperature of Earth's atmosphere due to increased levels of greenhouse gases

greenhouse gas
a substance in the air that traps heat in the atmosphere

predator
an animal that kills and eats other animals

LEARN MORE

Books

Marsh, Laura. *Polar Bears*. Washington, DC: National Geographic Kids, 2013.

Simon, Seymour. *Global Warming*. New York: HarperCollins, 2013.

Stirling, Ian. *Polar Bears: A Natural History of a Threatened Species*. Markham, ON: Fitzhenry & Whiteside, 2011.

Websites

To learn more about Bioindicator Species, visit **booklinks.abdopublishing.com**. These links are routinely monitored and updated to provide the most current information available.

Visit **mycorelibrary.com** for free additional tools for teachers and students.

INDEX

ABOUT THE AUTHOR

Tammy Gagne is the author of more than 100 books for adults and children. She resides in northern New England with her husband and son. One of her favorite pastimes is visiting schools to speak to kids about writing.